MW01242571

Christianity faces the 21st Century

(The Spirit, The Ballot Box, and the Pocketbook) by

Bill Wetterman

1

Table of Contents

Chapter 1

The Plague of Idolatry in America Today

grows daily. Most Christians living in America in the 21st Century agree that our country has not seen such turmoil and division in its history. A vast number of individuals in our nation view *truth* and *right* as *false* and *wrong*, and vice versa. Regardless of what religious denomination a person belongs, the rapid decline in standards of decency seems shocking to the average American.

These challenges to traditional Judeo-Christian values pit neighbor against neighbor, race against race, and worldview against worldview. As more Americans discard the past's ethics of civility, chaos reigns, and the divide grows.

The hatred of Christianity that sparks martyrdom around the world festers here in the United States, both in our politics and in the philosophy of multiculturalism. Thus, the possibility of violence against Christians and Jews in this country hovers ever closer—so close, in fact, that the United States may be one national election away from turning an ideological war into a violent civil war, with our very culture in jeopardy, as well as our lives.

Believers should not be surprised by the uptick in attacks by the entertainment community, the media, and the liberal political machine. These attacks are the symptoms of our country's moral decline, not the cause. Christians face spiritual warfare. They do not realize the spirit realm in which they are fighting and are thereby unprepared.

Am I unfair?

Well, ask yourself these questions. Which ideology carries the most passionate enthusiasm for its causes—the Liberals or the Conservatives? Why is the Christian community in America a passive observer like a third-string quarterback sitting on the bench while his team is behind by thirty points? And,

I'm not talking about protests or riots. I'm talking about avid commitment.

The United States is far from united, and it is time for individual citizens to decide whether they will follow the God of the Bible or the god of self-indulgence. How are Christians to respond to the radical changes in our society, knowing self-indulgence is today's idolatry?

Information gathered from the Pew Research Center exit polls,[1] the National Election Pool,[2] NBC,[3] and CNN news,[4] plus National Public Radio[5] over the past two decades shows no remarkable change in religious peoples' voting patterns. And one must ask, "Why not!"

A battle rages today between the Conservative position that the Bible and the Constitution should be interpreted as they were written, and those who believe the Bible and the Constitution are living documents subject to different interpretations to suit the society and times in which they are applied.

On one side are Biblical fundamentalists who consider the Bible the infallible Word of God and legal scholars: such as Clarence Thomas, who holds that the Constitution should be interpreted as written. On the other side, are Gnostics and Deists, who hold to the Progressive Humanist position that interpretations of the Bible change as society dictates and should be used as a guide, not as gospel. And legal experts like Ruth Bader Ginsberg who believe the same about the Constitution. The first honoring the godly principles on which the Constitution was built. The second changing its meaning as the culture demands.

As Christians, we believe God does not change. He is the same yesterday, today, and forever. Laws based on the Word of God should not change either.

Here is an example of the way humanists, liberal politicians, the entertainment industry, and the media work. Those who do not follow the Bible are sly. They offer a temporary carrot. "I'll give you a free..." Or, "You have a right..." But their promises never happen. Those who promise don't deliver. Instead, your personal security grows questionable. Drugs and violence enter your neighborhoods. Sin increases in every corner of American society.

When humans grab at empty promises and unrealistic dreams disguised as facts, society falls farther away from God and His blessings. Human reasoning is deceitful. Following God is the only way to joy and happiness. The people who promise you free everything bring abortion, the LGBTQ agenda, increased lawlessness, and many other iniquities with them. Look at the programs supported by the Liberal agenda.

Just as with Eve in the Garden of Eden, the devil, Satan, today uses three effective tactics. First, deflection. He minimizes his own faults. Then, projection. He projects lies upon the person he is attacking. In the case of Eve, he is attacking the character of God. Finally, he promises a rich reward for breaking God's command. The serpent tells a lie.

> The serpent was the craftiest of all the creatures the Lord God had made. So, the serpent came to the woman. "Really?" he asked. "None of the fruit in the garden? God says you mustn't eat any of it?" Genesis 3:1 Living Bible

Eve corrects him.

> "Of course, we may eat it," the woman told him. "It's only the fruit from the tree at the center of the garden that we are not to eat. God says we mustn't eat it or even touch it, or we will die." Genesis 3:2-3

Eve misquotes the Lord God. He never told Adam that he could not touch the tree. Now the devil knows how misinformed Eve is. He projects the sin of lying onto God.

"That's a lie!" the serpent hissed. "You'll not die!"
Genesis 3:4

Finally, the serpent makes the false promise of a great reward.

"God knows very well that the instant you eat it you will become like him, for your eyes will be opened—you will be able to distinguish good from evil!" Genesis 3:5

First, deflect. Second, project. Then make a false promise. Humans under Satan's influence use the same technique repeatedly, and they do not even know they are deceived.

These are the tactics used to blind people into believing the lies of educators, politicians, and the media.

Chapter 2

Who are the Born-again Christians, the Lukewarm Churchgoers, and the Pagans?

Growing up, I was taught the United States was a Christian country. But in these confusing times, defining who a Christian is takes some explanation. The simplest way to establish whether a person is a Christian is whether they are part of the Body of Christ. In the Book of the Revelation, John described two types of churches that will claim to be followers of Jesus, the Messiah, as the End Times approach— The Church at Laodicea, the Lukewarm Church, and the Church at Philadelphia, the Born-again Church.

John described the Church at Laodicea as the Lord showed him.

> "I know you well—you are neither hot nor cold; I wish you were one or the other! [16] But since you are merely lukewarm, I will spit you out of my mouth!
> [17] "You say, 'I am rich, with everything I want; I don't need a thing!' And you don't realize that spiritually

you are wretched and miserable and poor and blind and naked." Revelation 3:15-17

Jesus told John to write about the Church at Philadelphia,

"I know you well; you aren't strong, but you have tried to obey and have not denied my Name. Therefore, I have opened a door to you that no one can shut.

9   "Note this: I will force those supporting the causes of Satan while claiming to be mine (but they aren't—they are lying) to fall at your feet and acknowledge that you are the ones I love.

10   "Because you have patiently obeyed me despite the persecution, therefore I will protect you from the time of Great Tribulation and temptation, which will come upon the world to test everyone alive.[11] Look, I am coming soon! Hold tightly to the little strength you have—so that no one will take away your crown.

[12] "As for the one who conquers, I will make him a pillar in the temple of my God; he will be secure and will go out no more; and I will write my God's Name on him, and he will be a citizen in the city of my God—the New Jerusalem, coming down from heaven from my God; and he will have my new Name inscribed upon him."
Revelation 3:8-12

So, I ask you, dear reader, in which church do you dwell? Have you made your commitment to stand with Christ and hold on to your faith in Him, or are you "lukewarm" toward Him, standing with one foot in worldly doubt? Are you willing to die for your faith, lose everything you have, and withstand torture while proclaiming Jesus is Lord?

"Ridiculous!" you say? I believe the time is closer than you think when Christians will be faced with these choices! Are you, dear reader, born-again?

One who is born-again believes there is an omnipresent, omnipotent, omniscient God who created all things and will judge all mankind at the end of the World.

God is triune having three distinct persons— God the Father, the planner of all things, God the Son, the creator of the Father's plan, and God the Holy Spirit, the revealer of the Father's plan to His creation.

Evil is real and was found in Lucifer, known as Satan, and in rebellion, a third of the host of angels in heaven fell in disgrace to Earth.

Believers know that on Earth, Satan deceived Adam and Eve in the Garden of Eden. And humanity lost fellowship with God and eternal life in heaven without a redeemer to save us.

God the Father was not taken by surprise at these events! He is an omnipresent and all-knowing God. He created a plan to save mankind before He ever formed us. The idea was to send God the Son, Jesus, to earth to live a sinless life and die on the cross, thereby paying the price for our sins. Only God can satisfy the Law of God.

Jesus, God the Son, was fathered by the Holy Spirit and born of a virgin. He is the only one who can claim to be one hundred percent God and one hundred percent Man, thereby making Him worthy to repay Man's debt to God.

"For God so loved the world, that he gave his only begotten Son, that whosoever believeth on him should not perish, but have eternal life." John 3:16 NKJV.

Jesus fulfilled God's Law by His death on the cross and opened the gates for anyone to enter heaven who repents and believes in Him as the Son of God. Sin is no longer the issue. What matters is whether an individual believes that what God the Father did for Jesus by raising Him from the dead into everlasting life in Heaven, He will do for you.

Many believe, but few repent. Repentance means turning around your life. It means recognizing you are a sinner and giving up your ego, pride, and will to trust and follow God. Furthermore, a sinner must admit that he is wrong, and God is right. This act makes all the difference and makes you a child of God. Belief without repentance does not save you.

In the Book of James, the author emphasized this point along with the harm done to Christ by believers who said they were Christians but acted and lived like pagans.

"Dear brothers, what's the use of saying that you have faith and are Christians if you aren't proving it by helping others? Will that kind of faith save anyone? [15] If you have a friend who is in need of food and clothing, [16] and you say to him, "Well, good-bye and God bless you; stay warm and eat hearty," and then don't give him clothes or food, what good does that do?

[17] So you see, it isn't enough just to have faith. You must also do good to prove that you have it. Faith that doesn't show itself by good works is no faith at all—it is dead and useless.

[18] But someone may well argue, "You say the way to God is by faith alone, plus nothing; well, I say that good works are important too, for without good works you can't prove whether you have faith or not; but anyone can see that I have faith by the way I act."

[19] Are there still some among you who hold that "only believing" is enough? Believing in one God? Well, remember that the demons believe this too—so strongly that they tremble in terror! [20] Fool! When will you ever learn that "believing" is useless without doing what God wants you to? Faith that does not result in good deeds is not real faith." James 2:14-20, Living Bible

We cannot please God if we try to work our way to heaven without accepting Christ as Savior. But, once we believe He is God and put our fleshly ways aside, then our works while following Him count, and we are indeed saved. F.F. Bruce wrote,

"When love is the compelling power, there is no sense of strain or conflict or bondage in doing what is right: the man or woman who is compelled by Jesus' love and empowered by His Spirit will do the Will of God from His heart."[6]

Salvation is by faith in the work of Jesus, the Christ, the Son of God. It is a free gift. It cannot be earned by our own efforts. Once a person makes the profession of faith, his status changes. No longer in fear of hell, he becomes a servant of Jesus, his Master, and he will receive rewards or lose them based upon his service.

Those who truly repent and accept Jesus are known as the Body of Christ. Neither the church they attend nor the denomination they belong to is relevant. Repentance means the works we do are through the mind of Christ, not our own human logic. The Holy Spirit, the Word of God, and the Bible give us the mind of Christ.

Once born-again, the need to evangelize grows within. Knowing we are saved from eternal damnation, we evangelize because hell is real, and we follow God's desire that all men might be saved. Therefore, we keep preaching the *Good News*. For faith comes by hearing and hearing by the Word of God.

In the Gospel of Mark, Jesus commands,

> "And then he told them, "You are to go into all the world and preach the Good News to everyone, everywhere.[16]Those who believe and are baptized will be saved. But those who refuse to believe will be condemned. Mark 16:15-16

I will repeat these verses again later because the world needs to hear the Word. Notice that these verses do not say that those who bring good news are responsible for a person's salvation. When God calls us to witness, we are only accountable for preaching the good news.

Lukewarm people and pagans need our evangelism. Lukewarm church attendees and pagans look alike. They think in terms of human understanding instead of godly wisdom. "Lukewarm" people seek to do good, but they use human reasoning. Human reasoning produces nothing but evil, yet these deceived individuals do not know they are contributing nothing for God. They are like the Old Testament Jews Isaiah writes about.

> "But we are not godly; we are constant sinners and have been all our lives. Therefore, your wrath is heavy on us. How can such as we be saved? [6] We are all infected and impure with sin. When we put on our prized robes of righteousness, we find they are but filthy rags. Like autumn leaves, we fade, wither, and fall. And our sins, like the wind, sweep us away. [7] Yet no one calls upon your name or pleads with you for mercy. Therefore, you have turned away from us and turned us over to our sins."
> Isaiah 64:5-7

Lukewarm individuals know *about* Christ. They may even pray to Him; however, they have no relationship or fellowship with Him. They call themselves Christians because they were born into families that called themselves Christians. But they are not committed and are inclined to let social, political, and moral issues be determined by the pressures of the time they live in, not by the Bible and Jesus' teachings. The "lukewarm" do not reject Jesus outright, but they do not accept Him as their personal friend and savior.

Those of us who are born-again members of the Body of Christ must witness the gospel to pagans and the "lukewarm" alike. There should be no difference between how we approach a "lukewarm" person and a heathen. Leading them into the Body of Christ is our primary goal for both types.

The pagan, however, rejects Christ and the concept of a personal God. They shake their fists at the thought of being accountable for their rebellious behavior. In America, their errors are fueled by Hollywood, the political left, and the media. Their arguments weave grandiose solutions to the World's problems based on idealism and human reason, not fact. And their lies foster confusion and chaos. They are no different than humanity before the Flood.

> "Noah was a pleasure to the Lord. Here is the story of Noah: [9-10] He was the only truly righteous man living on the earth at that time. He tried always to conduct his affairs according to God's will. And he had three sons—Shem, Ham, and Japheth.
> [11] Meanwhile, the crime rate was rising rapidly across the earth, and, as seen by God, the world was rotten to the core.
> [12-13] As God observed how bad it was, and saw that all mankind was vicious and depraved, he said to Noah, "I have decided to destroy all mankind; for the earth is filled with crime because of man. Yes, I will destroy mankind from the earth." Genesis 6:8-13

This was the condition of Man right before the flood, and this is the condition of Man today. Every human is rotten to the core outside the Body of Christ—even those who think they are doing good. But God, loving as He is, continues to forgive, show mercy, and withhold His final judgment on humanity, giving men time to turn from their evil ways.

Those in the Body of Christ do sin and sometimes fail to repent. They lose their fellowship with God, but not their relationship and salvation. As in the story of the Prodigal Son, the Father opens His arms wide when His child repents. It is a perilous state to defy the Almighty. Yet, He forgives. David, King of Israel, was a murderer, an adulterer, and a liar. But David was quick to repent when called into account. God read David's heart and mind and called him precious.

To those who have fallen out of fellowship, the Bible says,

"For though once your heart was full of darkness, now it is full of light from the Lord, and your behavior should show it! [9] Because of this light within you, you should do only what is good and right and true.

[10] Learn as you go along what pleases the Lord. [11] Take no part in the worthless pleasures of evil and darkness, but instead, rebuke and expose them. [12] It would be shameful even to mention here those pleasures of darkness that the ungodly do. [13] But when you expose them, the light shines in upon their sin and shows it up, and when they see how wrong they really are, some of them may even become children of light! [14] That is why

God says in the Scriptures, "Awake, O sleeper, and rise up from the dead; and Christ shall give you light."
Ephesians 5:8-14

God waits with open arms, like the father of the Prodigal Son, to welcome back into fellowship His children who repent. Jesus taught the following to show us how the Father feels about us.

"I will go home to my father and say, "Father, I have sinned against both heaven and you, [19] and am no longer worthy of being called your son. Please take me on as a hired man."

[20] "So he returned home to his father. And while he was still a long distance away, his father saw him coming, and was filled with loving pity and ran and embraced him and kissed him.

[21] "His son said to him, 'Father, I have sinned against heaven and you, and am not worthy of being called your son—'

[22] "But his father said to the slaves, 'Quick! Bring the finest robe in the house and put it on him. And a jeweled ring for his finger, and shoes![23] And kill the calf we have in the fattening pen. We must celebrate with a feast, [24] for this son of mine was dead and has returned to life. He was lost and is found." Luke 15:18-24

God is patient and longsuffering. He will always forgive His children. But He will not put up with humanity's rebellion forever. True believers, hypocrites, and pagans have coexisted since Adam's Fall. Each time we humans reached a place of moral depravity, God saved the remnant of believers and started afresh. He did so during the Flood by saving Noah and his family. He did so at Sodom and Gomorrah by saving Lot and his daughters. Yet, even after God gave the children of Israel the promised land, they did not take it all and regressed into the age of the Judges. By the end of the Book of Judges, Israel had fallen away from God's Law.

"In those days, there was no king in Israel; everyone did what was right in his own eyes." Judges 21:25

Still, God did not destroy the people. Instead, He sent His Son to save them and us. Two thousand plus years have passed since Jesus died on the cross. All the prophecies regarding Israel and the Church Age have been fulfilled. Human society has deteriorated again into perversion, decadence, and egocentricity. This time, the Bible is clear, God will come back to judge. At the flood, God destroyed the Earth with water. Now, He will slay with fire those who oppose Him.

"First, I want to remind you that in the last days there will come scoffers who will do every wrong they can think of and laugh at the truth.[4] This will be their line of argument: "So Jesus promised to come back, did he? Then where is he? He'll never come! Why, as far back as anyone can remember, everything has remained exactly as it was since the first day of creation."

[5-6] They deliberately forget this fact: that God did destroy the world with a mighty flood long after he had made the heavens by the word of his command and had used the waters to form the earth and surround it. [7] And God has commanded that the earth and the heavens be stored away for a great bonfire at the judgment day, when all ungodly men will perish. [8] But don't forget this, dear friends, that a day or a thousand years from now is like tomorrow to the Lord." 2 Peter 3:3-8

These fools will be destroyed by fire at the Second Coming of Christ if, The Body of Christ cannot persuade them with the gospel.

> "I saw the Beast and, assembled with him, earth's kings and their armies, ready to make war against the One on the horse and his army. The Beast was taken, and with him, his puppet, the False Prophet, who used signs to dazzle and deceive those who had taken the mark of the Beast and worshiped his image. They were thrown alive, those two, into Lake Fire and Brimstone. The rest were killed by the sword of the One on the horse, the sword that comes from his mouth. All the birds held a feast on their flesh." Revelation 19:19-21

Think hard. Would you rather be in the Lord's army when He returns, or would you rather stay "lukewarm" or pagan and fight against Him? The only prophecies yet to be fulfilled deal with the Tribulation and the events of Christ's Second Coming. The time is short. Choose wisely.

Chapter 3

The Tower of Babel and the End of Days

appear alike to me. Mankind has spiraled down into

decadence from its high point at Pentecost when

God's gift of the Holy Spirit came to indwell the Body

of Christ. Today, human beings have become so

debased that our World resembles both the time of the

Flood and the Tower of Babel.

Proverbs tells us that there are seven things God

hates.

"For there are six things the Lord hates—no, seven: haughtiness, lying, murdering, plotting evil, eagerness to do wrong, a false witness, sowing discord among brothers." Proverbs 6:16-19

God hates all Sin, so why does Solomon point

out these seven. A proud look violates the first four

commandments by placing our own desires above

God's plan for us. Our desires become idols we put

before the command to honor God first. Satan's fall

was his pride. Humanities' fall is the same. The other

six things break the next six commandments and cause discord, murder, adultery, and fornication to spread sowing disharmony among the brethren and— keeping unbelievers from accepting God's gift of Grace.

What is happening today and what happened at the Tower of Babel are satanically inspired movements that alter the minds of all people on the earth. Liberals and humanists devise evil plans aimed at abolishing God from the society in which we live. Consequently, followers of these plans shed innocent blood throughout the World. Christians and Jews are attacked for their beliefs. Liberal advocates demand the removal of God from our schools using lies about Separation of Church and State and its origins and utilize the internet and the media to spread their doctrines.

As Christians, our fight is against satanic powers. We should love those who are Satan's puppets by preaching the gospel of Christ to them while despising the work they do on Satan's behalf.

Satan deceives millions making them marionettes doing his will. Through his followers, rumors and gossip are spread as truth. The ignorant buy into the lies. They tell those lies, and then say we, the Christians, are the liars. They use deflection, projection, and grand ideas.

Satan has set up false gods—Scientology, Idolatry, Humanism, and Human Science to fortify his lies and lead the masses astray. He uses the "big three," politicians, educators, and the media, to go after our youth through the public schools from kindergarten to universities teaching Liberalism and banning prayer wherever they can. The devil's cohorts outlaw speakers who disagree with their agenda and then call Christians racists when we disagree with them.

"For we are not fighting against people made of flesh and blood, but against persons without bodies—the evil rulers of the unseen world, those mighty satanic beings and great evil princes of darkness who rule this world; and against huge numbers of wicked spirits in the spirit world." Ephesians 6:12

What is our Tower of Babel today? It is the worldwide communications network designed to spread lies faster than ever before using the internet where everyone communicates in the same language. When Iran captured a British oil tanker in the Strait of Hormuz, July 20, 2019, the news reached Los Angeles in seconds. So, a media person can make up lies, and the lies cover the whole World in the twinkling of an eye.

The same worldwide communication network can be used for good to spread the gospel. Franklin Graham can raise money for Samaritans Purse via the same media, But, in contrast, every sin possible finds its champions on the internet. Satan's message promises that you are okay, as you are. And, no one should worry about hell if there is no God to put you there. Enjoy. Remove the bigoted Christians who oppose you from the face of the earth. No one will hold you accountable.

The sad part is that Satan has succeeded in doing this again and again. He fooled Eve and Adam when they ate of the Tree of Knowledge. He deceived the whole World so that, by the time of Noah, only eight souls were saved from the Flood. The pride of mankind ended in total destruction. You would think that after the Flood, humanity would have changed. But no. Sexual sin and licentious behavior led to the construction of the Tower of Babel.

"And Noah began to be a farmer, and he planted a vineyard. [21] Then he drank of the wine and was drunk and became uncovered in his tent. [22] And Ham, the father of Canaan, saw the nakedness of his father and told his two brothers outside. [23] But Shem and Japheth took a garment, laid it on both their shoulders and went backward and covered the nakedness of their father. Their faces were turned away, and they did not see their father's nakedness." Genesis 9:20-23

What did 'seeing his father uncovered in his tent' mean in the Old Testament? Some students of the Torah believe Ham had a homosexual relationship with his father.[22] I have a different theory based on Scripture. Ham had sexual relations with his father's wife.

> "The man who lies with his father's wife has uncovered his father's nakedness; both of them shall surely be put to death. Their blood *shall be* upon them." Leviticus 20:11, Modern Bible.

And again,

> "Cursed is the one who lies with his father's wife because he has uncovered his father's bed." Deuteronomy 27:20 NKJV

Jacob used a similar example for Reuben, who lost his inheritance by the same act.

> "Reuben, you are my firstborn, My might and the beginning of my strength, The excellency of dignity and the excellency of power. [4] Unstable as water, you shall not excel, Because you went up to your father's bed; Then you defiled it—He went up to my couch. " Genesis 49

Noah got drunk. Ham came into his tent and had sex with Noah's wife. Not necessarily Ham's mother, but perhaps a new wife he married afterward. Since Noah lived several hundred years after the flood, this is not beyond reason. Then Ham bragged about it to his brothers who covered their father while turning their heads, so as not to embarrass him further.

The result of this act was the birth of Canaan, which is why the curse fell on Canaan, who was the seed of this vile act, the son of Ham, and the grandson of Noah by Noah's wife.

The lineage of Ham also produced Nimrod, son of Cush, grandson of Noah.

"One of the descendants[j] of Cush was Nimrod, who became the first of the kings. [9] He was a mighty hunter, blessed of God, and his name became proverbial. People would speak of someone as being "like Nimrod—a mighty hunter, blessed of God." [10] The heart of his empire included Babel." Genesis 10:8-10, Living Bible

Note that the beginning of Nimrod's kingdom was Babel. A few centuries after Noah's death, the strongest men built empires and the age of Human Government began. God's commandment to Noah and his sons was, "Be fruitful and multiply and fill the earth." But mankind disobeyed God. They had not ventured out, and the earth was not being filled.

Instead, the people of Babel built a tower toward the heavens. The people all spoke the same language, and their civilization was highly advanced to be able to create such a site. Genesis reveals the pride of Man in rebellion toward God.

"The people who lived there began to talk about building a great city, with a temple-tower reaching to the skies—a proud, eternal monument to themselves.

"This will weld us together," they said, "and keep us from scattering all over the world." So, they made great piles of hard-burned brick, and collected bitumen to use as mortar.

[5] But when God came down to see the city and the tower mankind was making, [6] he said, "Look! If they are able to accomplish all this when they have just begun to exploit their linguistic and political unity, just think of what they will do later! Nothing will be unattainable for

them![7] Come, let us go down and give them different languages, so that they won't understand each other's words!"

[8] So, in that way, God scattered them all over the earth; and that ended the building of the city. [9]That is why the city was called Babel (meaning "confusion") because it was there that Jehovah confused them by giving them many languages, thus widely scattering them across the face of the earth." Genesis 11:3-9

How quickly the rebellious took control. These people were disobedient, prideful, and smart. When God said, "Nothing will be unattainable for them," these rebellious people might have advanced past where our technology is today if given a chance. Instead of giving glory to God for their deliverance from the Flood, they desired to make a name for themselves. But God, the Trinity, had no intention of giving them that chance.

God's purpose for mankind was to fill the whole earth and reign over it. Many souls were yet to be born before God's full plan was to be revealed. The generations from Shem to Abraham, from Abraham to Moses, and from Moses to Christ have filled the earth. Nations have risen and fallen. The Body of Christ has replaced the Jewish people as the spokespersons for God. But soon, the authority to speak for God will be returned to the Jewish people during the Tribulation. And this is one sign for this is evident as the Age of Grace comes to its end. Humans are rapidly duplicating the same kind of rebellious attitude as experienced at Babel. It is being fulfilled before our eyes.

The Apostle Paul foresaw how men would be in our time.

"You may as well know this too, Timothy, that in the last days it is going to be very difficult to be a Christian. [2] For people will love only themselves and their money; they will be proud and boastful, sneering at God, disobedient to their parents, ungrateful to them, and thoroughly bad. [3] They will be hardheaded and never give in to others; they will be constant liars and troublemakers and will think nothing of immorality. They will be rough and cruel, and sneer at those who try to be good. [4] They will betray their friends; they will be hotheaded, puffed up with pride, and prefer good times to worshiping God. [5] They will go to church, yes, but they won't really believe

anything they hear. Don't be taken in by people like that."
2 Timothy 3 1-5

Do I believe Satan has a master plan to destroy Christianity in America and throughout the World? The answer is obvious. Yes! Perilous times have come. We know the Tribulation is near as we see the prophecies in the Bible fulfilled before our eyes. What are we as Christians to do? We are to turn back from apathy and use the Holy Spirit within us to reach the lost before it is too late for them.

In the Spiritual realm, there are three types of people living on this earth. The saved, the ignorant, and the hardened of heart. The first type, the born-again, who belong to the Body of Christ, have been given this command.

"And then he told them, "You are to go into all the world and preach the Good News to everyone, everywhere. [16] Those who believe and are baptized will be saved. But those who refuse to believe will be condemned." Mark 16:15

To this end, those of us who are saved cannot stand in silence. Instead, starting with our children, we should preach the gospel. In our daily lives, we should teach Biblical principles. And as God leads us, we must respond to His urging by witnessing to the ignorant and the hardened of heart. By His sovereign will, He calls us alongside certain people to share the Good News.

To do this, we must be prepared.

"Last of all I want to remind you that your strength must come from the Lord's mighty power within you. [11] Put on all of God's armor so that you will be able to stand safe against all strategies and tricks of Satan. [12] For we are not fighting against people made of flesh and blood, but against persons without bodies—the evil rulers of the unseen world, those mighty satanic beings and great evil princes of darkness who rule this world; and against huge numbers of wicked spirits in the spirit world.

[13] So use every piece of God's armor to resist the enemy whenever he attacks, and when it is all over, you will still be standing up.

[14] But to do this, you will need the strong belt of truth and the breastplate of God's approval. [15] Wear shoes that are able to speed you on as you preach the Good News of peace with God. [16] In every battle you will need faith as

your shield to stop the fiery arrows aimed at you by Satan. [17] And you will need the helmet of salvation and the sword of the Spirit—which is the Word of God." Ephesians 6:10-17

We must witness with love for the sinner and hate for Sin. If John 3:16 is true that "God so loved the world that He gave His only Son that whosoever believes in Him will not perish but will have eternal life," then we must love each person enough to witness to them with the truth and help them understand that their eternal future is in jeopardy.

The second type of people are the ignorant. They need to be educated.

"Anyone who calls upon the name of the Lord will be saved.
[14] But how shall they ask him to save them unless they believe in him? And how can they believe in him if they have never heard about him? And how can they hear about him unless someone tells them? [15] And how will anyone go and tell them unless someone sends him? That is what the Scriptures are talking about when they say, 'How beautiful are the feet of those who preach the Gospel of peace with God and bring glad tidings of good things.'" Romans 10:13-15

Our own egos prevent us from speaking out because we fear we will fail. God does not require us to convert people. He expects us to voice His message so they may hear the gospel. Once they have listened, the choice is theirs.

> "Son of dust, if the people of a land sin against me, then I will crush them with my fist, break off their food supply, and send a famine to destroy both man and beast. [14] Even if Noah, Daniel, and Job were in it, they alone would be saved by their righteousness, and I would destroy the remainder of Israel," says the Lord God."
> Ezekiel 14:13-14

If Noah, Daniel, and Job by their presence could not deliver another human being, neither can you. The Spirit of God does that work. We will lose blessings at the Judgment Seat of Christ if we remain mute. If we speak, they will hear and cannot say they did not know.

Finally, there are those so hardened that they are seldom repentant. Although we must preach the gospel to them in love, we must also stand firm against their attacks on us. Think of Moses standing before Pharaoh. Think of Jesus standing before the Pharisees.

> "Lord, who will believe us? Who will accept God's mighty miracles as proof?" [39] But they couldn't believe, for as Isaiah also said: [40] "God has blinded their eyes and hardened their hearts so that they can neither see nor understand nor turn to me to heal them." [41] Isaiah was referring to Jesus when he made this prediction, for he had seen a vision of the Messiah's glory.
> [42] However, even many of the Jewish leaders believed him to be the Messiah but wouldn't admit it to anyone because of their fear that the Pharisees would excommunicate them from the synagogue; [43] for they loved the praise of men more than the praise of God."
> John 12:38-43

A better translation of "hardened their hearts" would be *allowed to harden their own hearts*.

Eventually, it will be with these people as it was with those in Noah's time, and Jesus will annihilate them upon His return.

"When the Lord God saw the extent of human wickedness, and that the trend and direction of men's lives were only towards evil, [6] he was sorry he had made them. It broke his heart.

[7] And he said, 'I will blot out from the face of the earth all mankind that I created.'" Genesis 6:5-7

Chapter 4

The Power of the Spirit of God resides within us. What does the Bible say we are to do before Jesus returns at the end of this the last age? Born-again Christians are to stand in the power of the Holy Spirit. Our strength is in our faithfulness and in our love for one another. Scripture says,

> "Last of all I want to remind you that your strength must come from the Lord's mighty power within you. [11] Put on all of God's armor so that you will be able to stand safe against all strategies and tricks of Satan." Ephesians 6:10-11

Notice what it does not say—fight. God will do the fighting for us. He will also do the judging! Bombing abortion clinics, destroying others' property, or supporting right-wing reactionaries is not the godly way for the Body of Believers to act. Instead, we are to promote the gospel. So that all mankind may hear of God's sacrifice and grace on our behalf and repent. Look at Mark 16 again.

> "And He said to them, "Go into all the world and preach the gospel to every creature.[16] He who believes and is baptized will be saved, but he who does not believe will be condemned." Mark 16:15-16

The Holy Spirit, who dwells within the Body of Christ, will give us the words to say when the time comes for each of us to speak out.

> "God means what he says. What he says goes. His powerful Word is sharp as a surgeon's scalpel, cutting through everything, whether doubt or defense, laying us open to listen and obey. Nothing and no one is impervious to God's Word. We can't get away from it—no matter what." Hebrews 4:12, The Message Bible.

The Holy Spirit will give us His words to speak, and His words will do the work. We must explore diligently to make those words part of our daily living. And to study means to delve into the Bible— study the Word of God. Paul said,

> "Be diligent to present yourself approved to God, a worker who does not need to be ashamed, rightly dividing the word of truth." 2 Timothy 2:15, NKJV

Paul commended the people of Berea as an example of how we should be when it comes to studying the Word.

> "They received the word with all readiness and searched the Scriptures daily to find out whether these things were so." Act 17:11

With the Holy Spirit as our guide, we can study the Scriptures with the mind of Christ and go back into the Old Testament to see for ourselves what was written about the plan of God for mankind. We can understand the prophecies and their fulfillment throughout the entire sixty-six books of the Bible.

Two of the gifts of the Holy Spirit are the gifts of teaching and preaching. Ministers with these gifts can help explain areas where there may be confusion.

"He handed out gifts of apostle, prophet, evangelist, and pastor-teacher to train Christ's followers in skilled servant work, working within Christ's body, the church, until we're all moving rhythmically and easily with each other, efficient and graceful in response to God's Son, fully mature adults, fully developed within and without, fully alive like Christ." Ephesians 4:10, Message Bible

With the Holy Spirit, teachers can search the Scriptures and, with prayer and humility, be led to God's truth ignoring their own human understanding, which produces false doctrine.

"Don't be in any rush to become a teacher, my friends. Teaching is highly responsible work. Teachers are held to the strictest standards. And none of us is perfectly qualified." James 3:1-2

When we rely on our own strength, we cannot teach correctly. But, since every member of the Body of Christ has received the Holy Spirit, each has been equipped with the grace and the words to witness to the lost. Our job is not to point out other people's faults. We are to teach and preach to them what the Word of God says. God has given us His power and our voice to testify to the World. If we do this in love, many will hear and believe. Many will not. It is not our job to save them. It is our job to see that they understand, whether they accept…or not.

> "But I say, have they not heard? Yes, indeed: "Their voice went into all the earth, and their words to the ends of the world." Romans 10:18, NKJV

Chapter 5

Voting for the Bible or Voting for Humanism? Why do many Catholic voters ignore the teachings of their faith and of the Bible regarding abortion and homosexuality by voting with the liberal-progressive agenda? Catholics make up about a quarter of the electorate. Yet, in the 2016 election, Hispanic Catholics voted for candidates opposing their church's positions, over two to one. The reason had to do with social matters related to families and their communities. Those who put these issues ahead of the Word of God are unaware of the future consequences their vote will bring.

Remember, Satan's formula. Deflect, project, and make false promises. Understand one more thing. Progressives are all about keeping power and control over others. Once in authority, they propose tax increases, regulations that restrict freedoms like gun controls and healthcare that restricts choice. These individuals imagine unattainable dreams. Everybody should have free healthcare and money to buy what they want, even if they do not work. Yet II Thessalonians 3:10 says, "If anyone will not work, neither shall he eat."

Progressives boast that mankind can solve the earth's pollution problems. Human beings without God are easily swayed to believe these lies. Humanity has never solved a social problem through human reasoning. Why not? Because when two people are placed in a room, they will end up arguing over something. Multiply them by the nearly eight billion humans roaming the face of the earth, and the chances of humanity agreeing on any one issue are impossible.

To maintain power, those who have it lie out of ignorance. These elitists tell untruths about their enemies and offer grand solutions to non-existent problems. Their ideas sound attractive, but they bring discord, poverty, and fear with them because they oppose the biblical teachings of God. Progressives promise peace and equality for everyone while ignoring God's Word. And evil is the result in the long run. In 1st Thessalonians, the Scripture reads,

"For when they say, "Peace and safety!" then sudden destruction comes upon them, as labor pains upon a pregnant woman. And they shall not escape. ⁴But you, brethren, are not in darkness, so that this Day should overtake you as a thief. 1st Thessalonians 5:3-4.

Born-again Christians must believe the Bible and see the destruction that is coming.

Jewish voters fall for the progressives' lies as well. If they did not learn from the Tree of Life synagogue massacre or the Obama administration's dislike of the State of Israel,[7] then, they should have learned something by listening to American minister Louis Farrakhan, the leader of the religious group, Nation of Islam, and the pro-Palestinian radical leftists like Ilhan Omar.[8]

But to date, Jewish voters continue to vote for the leftist-progressive movement three to one. Do they want to see another annihilation attempt occur in their own lifetimes? Are they ill-informed? Anti-Semites like Louis Farrakhan practice *'the seven things God hates'* seen in Proverbs 6:16-19.

I can imagine only three possibilities for their voting preferences. Some Jewish voters do not believe in the tenets of their faith or in the God of Abraham anymore. Many ignore their lineage in favor of fame, money, and celebrity, or some Jewish voters cannot break with the voting traditions of their fathers. Regardless of their reasons, the results are devastating. Anti-Semitism is growing, and Islamists are being elected in liberal districts and are condemning Israel.

To be a Jew in America and vote with the leftist-liberal agenda seems demonically inspired to me. Given the history of genocide through the ages against them, Jews should be seriously concerned about the consequences of their vote in support of progressive causes.

The Bible tells us the truth. Many Jews have reject Biblical truth. While the Jewish people had produced great thinkers over the centuries, human reasoning has guided their conclusions, not the Word of God. So, they have rejected the teachings of God throughout the history of the Bible—Abraham, Moses, David, and the prophets.

> "My people are destroyed for lack of knowledge: because thou hast rejected knowledge, I will also reject thee, that thou shalt be no priest to me: seeing thou hast forgotten the law of thy God, I will also forget thy children." Hosea 4:6

For centuries, false priests and prophets have misled the Jewish people by rejecting God's knowledge and replacing it with their own. It is time for Jewish voters to wake up to Satan's attack on them before it is too late.

The trend of apathy among Black voters had increased as well. In 2016 Black voters represented twelve percent of the electorate, less than in the Obama years, because over a million stayed home rather than vote.[4,5] Exit polling from Edison Media Research via Roper Center showed that those who voted in support of the Liberal agenda dropped five percent but remained close to eighty-eight percent.[4,5]

Cultural issues like racial prejudice, unequal treatment under the law, and poverty drive these voters. Significant as these issues are, they should not override the biblical violations that the liberal agenda fosters through them. As a race, Black Americans in the United States have been courted by the Left-wing, who promised to improve the situation for Blacks. Seldom does anything change. Where do the promises go once the election is over? They are put away until the next election year.

Our role as the Body of Christ is to love the person and desire God's best for everyone. Jesus died for all men, and all men are sinners. The term 'all men' means precisely what it says. He wants every person with a soul—Black, White, Male, Female, Homosexual—to be saved and come to the true faith in Jesus, the Christ. But we cannot let our own fleshly thinking hinder the message by supporting the Liberal agenda.

Among those who identify as born-again evangelicals, over fifteen percent voted for Liberal candidates in the 2016 election defying Godly reason.[1,2,3,4,5] What deceives them is the access to media, which skews truth into half-truths and puts glamourous tones on falsehoods. I have heard fellow Christians say, "I don't like the looks of that guy," rather than examining the voting record of results in the candidate's past.

"Then if anyone says to you, 'Look, here is the Christ!' or 'There!' do not believe it. [24] For false christs and false prophets will rise and show great signs and wonders to deceive, if possible, even the elect. [25] See, I have told you beforehand." Matthew 24:23-25.

Many luminaries today proclaim to have the answer to all our problems. They look and talk like angels of light, but behind their smiles lies the pit of hell. Take care, my brothers and sisters, that you are not deceived.

Chapter 6

The Bible and the Constitution Are Linked. From the same Pew Study cited in Chapter 1, the facts show that more Liberals than Conservatives are likely to be born outside of the United States.[1] They do not go to church and have a higher percentage of unmarried individuals. This flies in the face of the Judeo/Christian principles and beliefs of our founding fathers. Those who claim the ultra-left agenda do not desire to conform to the ideologies that formed our country. They do not assimilate but rather impose on our society the cultures from which they came, unlike the immigrants before them.

The Bible and the Constitution are bonded together by the beliefs of the founders.

Here are quotes from some of the leaders of our country in the early stages of its development.

In his General Orders, May2, 1778, George Washington wrote.

> "While we are zealously performing the duties of good citizens and soldiers, we certainly ought not to be inattentive to the higher duties of religion. To the distinguished character of Patriot, it should be our highest glory to add the more distinguished character of Christian."[2]

John Adams wrote to Thomas Jefferson, 28 June 1813.

> "Now I will avow, that I then believe, and now believe, that those general Principles of Christianity, are as eternal and immutable, as the Existence and Attributes of God; and that those Principles of Liberty, are as unalterable as human Nature and our terrestrial, mundane System." [9]

The argument that the Separation of Church and State means the abolition of any religious profession in decision making by local, state, and national government is absurd. Our Nation's first textbooks were Biblically based. Most of our eighteenth and early nineteenth-century schools and institutions were founded by religious denominations.

The First Amendment, which was ratified in 1791, states that "Congress shall make no law respecting an establishment of religion or prohibiting the free exercise thereof." However, the phrase "separation of church and state" itself does not appear in the United States Constitution.

Great Britain's government has no provisions regarding the separation of church and state. The Church of England sustains a traditional Catholic order system that includes ordained bishops, priests, and deacons. The Church follows an episcopal form of government. It is divided into two provinces: Canterbury and York. The Church's bishops play a lawmaking role in Britain. Several seats in the House of Lord's are held by bishops of The Church of England, and the monarch is considered the head of the church. Britain's form of government is what our

Constitution prohibits.[10]

The scars of abuse from centuries past prompted Congress to assure that no one religion ever locked itself to the legislative process. There is a difference between the establishment of a State religion and the practicing of the Christian faith, which in the eighteenth and nineteenth century was the cornerstone belief of ninety-nine percent of our citizens and the primary teaching materials for our school systems at all levels of learning.

In John Hancock's Provincial Resolution to Massachusetts Bay, October 1774, he writes.

"Resistance to tyranny becomes the Christian and social duty of each individual. ... Continue steadfast and, with a proper sense of your dependence on God, nobly defend those rights which heaven gave, and no man ought to take from us." From *The Life of John Quincy Adams*, page 248,

"The hope of a Christian is inseparable from his faith. Whoever believes in the divine inspiration of the Holy Scriptures must hope that the religion of Jesus shall prevail throughout the earth. Never since the foundation of the world have the prospects of mankind been more encouraging to that hope than they appear to be at the present time. And may the associated distribution of the

Bible proceed and prosper till the Lord shall have made 'bare His holy arm in the eyes of all the nations, and all the ends of the earth shall see the salvation of our God' (Isaiah 52:10)."[9]

The hope of a Christian is not in religion, like being a Catholic, Protestant, or member of any other dominant religion of the World. It is the belief in the deity of the Son of God and His ability to save our souls, forgive our sins, and grant us eternal life. I could go on with quotes from most of the signers of the Declaration of Independence. But I will only add one more. Even the deists of the time agreed our nation was founded on Christian beliefs and principles.

Benjamin Franklin wrote this in a letter to Ezra Stiles, President of Yale University, on March 9, 1790.

"I believe in one God, the Creator of the Universe. That He governs it by His Providence. That He ought to be worshipped...As to Jesus of Nazareth, my opinion of whom you particularly desire, I think the system of morals and his religion, as he left them to us, is the best the world ever saw, or is likely to see.[9]

The Liberal wave in the United States today comes in part from immigrants who are not inclined to neither adopt our religious beliefs nor the principles of conduct that these beliefs are based upon. They find support from a group of elitists who advocate the abolishment of nationalism in favor of a one-World government. The planned drive to move the United States toward a globalist, and/or at least a socialist country, must be halted by the uniting of true Christian believers in vocal opposition. Our disapproval must be shown by using the power of the ballot box and casting our votes against this growing tide.

We must also use our pocketbooks to remove our wealth from venues that these elitists own and operate.

Chapter 7

Exposing Lies and Preaching the Gospel

to save the lost is the primary objective of The Body of Christ. Wasn't pride the platform Satan used to base his case for opposing God? Satan's ego was his downfall. The Scripture says,

> "How you are fallen from heaven, O Lucifer, son of the morning! How you are cut down to the ground—mighty though you were against the nations of the world. [13] For you said to yourself, "I will ascend to heaven and rule the angels.[a] I will take the highest throne. I will preside on the Mount of Assembly far away in the north.* [14] I will climb to the highest heavens and be like the Most High." [15] But instead, you will be brought down to the pit of hell, down to its lowest depths. [16] Everyone there will stare at you and ask, "Can this be the one who shook the earth and the kingdoms of the world? [17] Can this be the one who destroyed the world and made it into a shamble, who demolished its greatest cities and had no mercy on his prisoners?" Isaiah 14:12-17, Living Bible

Satan's tools to accomplish his plans are deceit, deflection, projection, and false promises. Deceit fools unsaved people as well as Christians who follow their flesh and not their Lord. America is being deceived into thinking what used to be considered evil is now right. And right is now wrong.

Jesus confronted the deceit of Satan's followers in His own time.

> "For you are the children of your father the devil, and you love to do the evil things he does. He was a murderer from the beginning and a hater of truth—there is not an iota of truth in him. When he lies, it is perfectly normal, for he is the father of liars.[45] And so when I tell the truth, you just naturally don't believe it! John 8:44-45

People believe the lies Satan plants saying there is no God and no hell. Yet Jesus preached about hell more than he did heaven. Why? Because he didn't want anyone to go there. The Bible mentions hell fifty-four times. It is a place of hopelessness and flames.

Here is one example.

> "There was a certain rich man," Jesus said, "who was splendidly clothed and lived each day in mirth and luxury. [20] One day Lazarus, a diseased beggar, was laid at

his door. [21] As he lay there longing for scraps from the rich man's table, the dogs would come and lick his open sores. [22] Finally, the beggar died and was carried by the angels to be with Abraham in the place of the righteous dead.[c] The rich man also died and was buried, [23] and his soul went into hell.[d] There, in torment, he saw Lazarus in the far distance with Abraham. [24] "'Father Abraham,' he shouted, 'have some pity! Send Lazarus over here if only to dip the tip of his finger in water and cool my tongue, for I am in anguish in these flames.'

[25] "But Abraham said to him, 'Son, remember that during your lifetime you had everything you wanted, and Lazarus had nothing. So now he is here being comforted, and you are in anguish. [26] And besides, there is a great chasm separating us, and anyone wanting to come to you from here is stopped at its edge; and no one over there can cross to us.'

[27] "Then the rich man said, 'O Father Abraham, then please send him to my father's home— [28] for I have five brothers—to warn them about this place of torment lest they come here when they die.'

[29] "But Abraham said, 'The Scriptures have warned them again and again. Your brothers can read them any time they want to.'

[30] "The rich man replied, 'No, Father Abraham, they won't bother to read them. But if someone is sent to them from the dead, then they will turn from their sins.'

[31] "But Abraham said, 'If they won't listen to Moses and the prophets, they won't listen even though someone rises from the dead.'" Luke 16:19-31

Unbelievers reject the concept of Hell because they want no one to judge them. They forget God is a just God. For the vast number of people, the pathway to eternal damnation is being sauntered down unawares. They shake their fists against God because they cannot accept the fact that, on the day of their death, they must account for their actions to Him.

Here is what the Bible says it will be like in our time.

> "Look here, you rich men, now is the time to cry and groan with anguished grief because of all the terrible troubles ahead of you. [2] Your wealth is even now rotting away, and your fine clothes are becoming mere motheaten rags. [3] The value of your gold and silver is dropping fast, yet it will stand as evidence against you and eat your flesh like fire. That is what you have stored up for yourselves to receive on that coming day of judgment... [5] You have spent your years here on earth having fun, satisfying your every whim, and now your fat hearts are ready for the slaughter. [6] You have condemned and killed good men who had no power to defend themselves against you."
> James 5:1-6.

Christians are appalled by the evil present in this age. But we should be even more shocked by the eternal damnation that awaits so many unaware. Unbelievers go after false gods and worldly idols, rejecting the thought that they will someday be held accountable whether in this World or in the next. Their only hope is to receive Jesus as their Lord and Savior. Otherwise, they will perish while they live and after they die.

> "No one is good—no one in all the world is innocent." [11] No one has ever really followed God's paths or even truly wanted to.[12] Everyone has turned away; all have gone wrong. No one anywhere has kept on doing what is right, not one.
> [13] Their talk is foul and filthy like the stench from an open grave. Their tongues are loaded with lies. Everything they say has in it the sting and poison of deadly snakes.
> [14] Their mouths are full of cursing and bitterness. [15] They are quick to kill, hating anyone who disagrees with them. [16] Wherever they go they leave misery and trouble behind them, [17] and they have never known what it is to feel secure or enjoy God's blessing.
> [18] They care nothing about God nor what he thinks of them. Romans 3:10-18.

This is the real state of mankind without God. All individuals must be reached with the gospel of Christ before the reality of Hell faces them.

Even within so-called Christian Evangelical circles, we must beware today of services where coffee and donuts are more important than the Word of God. Where the gospel is watered down, so people seeking social acceptance will not be offended by God's truth. Peter warns us of this.

> "But there were false prophets, too, in those days, just as there will be false teachers among you. They will cleverly tell their lies about God, turning against even their Master who bought them, but theirs will be a swift and terrible end. [2] Many will follow their evil teaching that there is nothing wrong with sexual sin. And because of them Christ and his way will be scoffed at.
> [3] These teachers in their greed will tell you anything to get hold of your money. But God condemned them long ago and their destruction is on the way… [19] "You aren't saved by being good," they say, "so you might as well be bad. Do what you like; be free."
> But these very teachers who offer this "freedom" from the law are themselves slaves to sin and destruction. For a man is a slave to whatever controls him." 2 Peter 2:1-3, 19

There are many churches today who boast of being Christian in faith, settling for a watered-down gospel to increase membership and not calling sin out for what it is. They weaken the cause of Christ and carry eternal consequences for those who follow their teaching.

Why is the Liberal ideology so attractive to human beings? Why are people drawn to Scientology, Mysticism, Atheism, and Humanism?

Because, if there is a Just God, He will hold them accountable for their actions. The God of the Bible, both the Old and the New Testaments, is both a God of Grace and a God of Justice. Human pride is being encouraged by Satanic forces to believe as the poet says, "I am the master of my fate. I am the captain of my soul."

If God does not exist, or, if God created us, and then vanished to create other worlds, who is left to hold mankind accountable?

Born-again Christians cannot ignore what is occurring in America. Born-again Christians must vote for candidates who align themselves with the Holy Bible and not the World. God loves all and wishes for no one to perish in Hell. So, we should love all people enough to stand firm on the Bible in the hopes of winning the lost though they may rage at us.

I have seen firsthand the power of God to turn what seemed an impossible situation into a glorious victory. My home church was several million dollars in debt. Our pastor had a vision that we would sell our property, pay off that debt, and go into our new church in good financial shape. We prayed for four and a half years as a congregation, and privately, and God came through. God will do the same thing for America.

We are in a place in our country like Israel was in the time of the Judges.

"In those days there was no king in Israel, but every man did that which was right in his own eyes." Judges 17:6, NKJV

America has turned its back on our Savior. Everyone is doing what seems right in their own eyes.

But God says.

"If my people, which are called by my name, shall humble themselves, and pray, and seek my face, and turn from their wicked ways; then will I hear from heaven, and will forgive their sin, and will heal their land." 2 Chronicles 7:14

The time has come for prayer groups, whole congregations, all true Christian believers and their leaders to pray daily, earnestly, and unceasingly for the restoration of America back to the faith that created this country. Prayer and submission to God's Word and commandments can still heal our land.

"And we are sure of this, that he will listen to us whenever we ask him for anything in line with his will. [15] And if we really know he is listening when we talk to him and make our requests, then we can be sure that he will answer us." 1st John 5:14-15, Living Bible.

"Remember that the Lord is coming soon. [6] Don't worry about anything; instead, pray about everything; tell God your needs, and don't forget to thank him for his answers. [7] If you do this, you will experience God's peace, which is far more wonderful than the human mind can understand. His peace will keep your thoughts and your hearts quiet and at rest as you trust in Christ Jesus. Philippians 4:5-7

The way prayer is shown in these verses demonstrates how we are to pray. We are to ask, according to His Will. God will neither honor prayer that violates His laws and covenants nor honor requests that oppose His Will. He is sovereign. Christians are to pray, believing that He will stand by His Word and His promises. And then, we are to walk in things that are honest, just, and praiseworthy as we wait for our prayers to be answered.

Further, Christians should pray specifically as the Bible states we should and for the purposes outlined in Scripture.

One of those purposes is so we can freely preach the gospel. We know rulers hold power because God allows them. Jesus verifies this in the Gospel of John.

"You won't talk to me?" Pilate demanded. "Don't you realize that I have the power to release you or to crucify you?"

[11] Then Jesus said, "You would have no power at all over me unless it were given to you from above. So those[a] who brought me to you have the greater sin." John 19:10-11, Modern English Version

Paul clarifies that rulers remain in power when they enforce laws that align with the Bible.

"Obey the government, for God is the one who has put it there. There is no government anywhere that God has not placed in power. [2] So those who refuse to obey the laws of the land are refusing to obey God, and punishment will follow. [3] For the policeman does not frighten people who are doing right; but those doing evil will always fear him. So if you don't want to be afraid, keep the laws and you will get along well. [4] The policeman is sent by God to help you. But if you are doing something wrong, of course, you should be afraid, for he will have you punished. He is sent by God for that very purpose. [5] Obey the laws, then, for two reasons: first, to keep from being punished, and second, just because you know you should." Romans 13:1-5

Our rulers should reinforce God's laws and commandments, and when they do, offenders should be afraid because justice is from God. Our job as Christians is to obey laws in line with the Bible.

In fact, Paul tells us why.

"Therefore I exhort first of all that you make supplications, prayers, intercessions, and thanksgivings for everyone, for kings, and for all that are in authority; that we may lead a quiet and peaceable life in all godliness and honesty." 1 Timothy 2:1-2

Why are we to pray for our leaders? So that we may live our lives peacefully and spread the gospel unafraid.

And, leaders should study carefully how they rule because God has the power to remove them.

"For promotion and power come from nowhere on earth, but only from God. He promotes one and deposes another. Psalm 75:5, Living Bible

"Blessed be the name of God forever and ever, for he alone has all wisdom and all power. [21] World events are under his control. He removes kings and sets others on their thrones." Daniel 2:20-21

And God has done this throughout history. When God found Saul unfit to be king, He removed him.

"Finally, the Lord said to Samuel, "You have mourned long enough for Saul, for I have rejected him as king of Israel. Now take a vial of olive oil and go to Bethlehem and find a man named Jesse, for I have selected one of his sons to be the new king." 1st Samuel 16:1

When God found Belshazzar too wicked to rule, He removed him.

"But you have not praised the God who gives you the breath of life and controls your destiny! 24 25 And so God sent those fingers to write this message: 'Mene,' 'Mene,' 'Tekel,' 'Parsin.' 26

"This is what it means:

"Mene means 'numbered'—God has numbered the days of your reign, and they are ended.

27 "Tekel means 'weighed'—you have been weighed in God's balances and have failed the test.

28 "Parsin means 'divided'—your kingdom will be divided and given to the Medes and Persians." Daniel 5:23-28.

God is sovereign. Leaders rule by His will. Our prayers can keep good rulers in power and remove the ungodly.

Chapter 8

Voting Issues with Biblical Significance

need close attention. Remember these facts. Satan uses social discontent as a wedge to bring chaos into human societies. His followers lie, deflect their own lies by projecting the people of God as the real liars and promise grandiose plans to solve the problems of poverty, inequality, and prejudice. But his followers never deliver on those promises.

I will touch on a few of the major issues facing Americans today. We will see the differences between God's position on these issues and humanists' views. The comparisons are startlingly clear. Born-again Christians must use the power of the ballot box to support God's Word.

The Right to Life is a significant issue facing Christians. Today in America, we murder unborn children because of the lies of Satan and the pride of

Man. Abortion violates many laws of God. I will select only a few of the Scriptures that show God's hatred of both the sins of immorality that cause women to seek abortions and the murder of innocents that abortion indeed is.

At the beginning of the Bible, God states His will for mankind.

> "So God created man in his own image, in the image of God created he him; male and female created he them. [28] And God blessed them, and God said unto them, Be fruitful, and multiply, and replenish the earth, and subdue it." Genesis 1:27-28, NKJV.

Since we are created in God's image, He instructs us to be fruitful and multiply. The reproduction of life is commanded. It is more than a right. God tells Noah the same thing before the Flood. Here God adds that murder is forbidden and has consequences.

Any man who murders shall be killed; for to kill a man is to kill one made like God. [7] Yes, have many children and repopulate the earth and subdue it." Genesis 9:6-7

Sex is meant to be between one man and one woman. Today, society rejects this idea. People live together without being married, and the term *'significant other'* is tossed around with impunity. But God says in Genesis,

"Her name is 'woman' because she was taken out of a man." [24] This explains why a man leaves his father and mother and is joined to his wife in such a way that the two become one person." Genesis 2:24 Living Bible.

The Commandment of God says in Exodus 20:14, "Thou shalt not commit adultery." King James Version.

Clearly, any sexual relationship other than within marriage between a man and a woman is Sin. The life created by the union of a husband and wife is precious in God's sight. Taking that life, even by accident, has its penalty.

"When there's a fight, and in the fight a pregnant woman is hit so that she miscarries but is not otherwise hurt, the one responsible has to pay whatever the husband demands in compensation." Exodus 21:22-23, Message Bible.

God is omnipresent. Meaning, He is always everywhere at once. God knows every human life that was, is, and will be created. He sees each life as a living soul and spirit with a purpose. What right does mankind have to abort God's living soul?

"Before I shaped you in the womb, I knew all about you. Before you saw the light of day, I had holy plans for you." Jeremiah 1:5.

Those who believe that it is all right to abort a fetus because it isn't human forget about God's genetics. If the embryo isn't human, why do anything at all? Sex creates a living soul. Killing that soul is murder. The lies Satan spreads through his followers say it is all right to get rid of an unwanted child. God disagrees. A human is a human when the sperm enters the egg. God says so. He also says if you injure that life intentionally, there will be consequences.

In the Old Testament, Israel adopted pagan practices. One of them was burning their children as sacrifices to idols.

"Son of dust, you must accuse Jerusalem and Samaria of all their awful deeds. [37] For they have committed both adultery and murder; they have worshiped idols and murdered my children whom they bore to me, burning them as sacrifices on their altars. [38] On the same day they defiled my Temple and ignored my Sabbaths, [39] for when they had murdered their children in front of their idols, then even that same day they actually came into my Temple to worship! That is how much regard they have for me!" Ezekiel 23:36-38, The Living Bible.

Today, we abort our children as a sacrifice to the gods of decadence.

Most abortions today are for convenience and are the result of violations of the sixth commandment of God. Women say, "Having a baby would dramatically change my life." "I can't afford a baby now." "I don't want a child with that man." "Raising a child will interfere with my education."

Americans are murdering their children because of a life of fornication and sexual immorality. And they are given the right to kill by our court system and our politicians. With today's technology—birth control methods and the like—even people living in sin can avoid pregnancy. But they don't. They gratify their own lusts and then murder the innocent.

Hebrews 13:4 "Marriage is honorable in all and the bed undefiled. But whoremongers and adulterers, God will judge." Hebrews 13:4 NKJV

When we consider how many citizens of the United States are living together outside the bonds of marriage, we must consider the consequences for our country. When you go to the polls to vote, don't vote for a political party. Instead, study the candidates' positions beforehand like the Bereans studied the Scripture, and vote for a candidate that supports life from a Biblical standpoint. Just because a candidate looks good, promises a grand future, and claims to have the answers to today's problems, does not mean they will make Biblical choices when in office. Study their records. Know who you are voting for.

Homosexuality and the LGBTQ Community is another equally vital issue facing Christians in the United States today, along with The Right to Life.

Given the LGBTQ community's revisionist approach to history and morality, their demand for legitimacy, both socially and politically, poses an ethical problem.

Here are examples of how the LGBTQ community attempts at justification. First, they say Christians misinterpret the Scripture.

"The story of Sodom and Gomorrah in Genesis 19 is well known. This is where the terms "sodomite" and "sodomy" originate, and it has long been associated with biblical condemnation of male homosexual sex. It is, however, actually about gang-rape."[11]

Excuse me? Who is misinterpreting? Here is the actual Scripture.

"And they called to Lot and said to him, "Where are the men who came to you tonight? Bring them out to us that we may know them carnally." Genesis 19:5

They wanted to gang rape, yes, but they desired a homosexual gang rape. Lot offered them his two unmarried daughters. But they refused.

"Lot went out, barring the door behind him, and said, "Brothers, please, don't be vile! Look, I have two daughters, virgins; let me bring them out; you can take your pleasure with them, but don't touch these men—they're my guests.
⁹ They said, "Get lost! You drop in from nowhere, and now you're going to tell us how to run our lives. We'll treat you worse than them!" And they charged past Lot to break down the door.
10-11 But the two men reached out and pulled Lot inside the house, locking the door." Genesis 19:6-10.

The claim that this was not a homosexual act does not hold with Scripture.

Here is a second justification used by the LGBTQ community. Jesus didn't speak about same-sex marriage, so he is at least neutral if not open to it. What Jesus did not condemn, we should not condemn. Paul clarifies this issue in 1 Corinthians.

> "Don't you know that those doing such things have no share in the Kingdom of God? Don't fool yourselves. Those who live immoral lives, who are idol worshipers, adulterers or homosexuals—will have no share in his Kingdom. Neither will thieves or greedy people, drunkards, slanderers, or robbers. [11] There was a time when some of you were just like that but now your sins are washed away, and you are set apart for God, and he has accepted you because of what the Lord Jesus Christ and the Spirit of our God have done for you." 1 Corinthians 6:9-11, Living Bible.

Here is the catch. Mankind is guilty of all sorts of Sin. Saved people are sinners, but they recognize Sin for what it is and repent of it. They may slip and fall, but they ask for and receive forgiveness. Whereas people who say I am the way I am, and God understands, deceive themselves and remain in their sin. Nowhere in Scripture is homosexuality condoned.

A third justification is, "God made me this way." A presidential candidate has said he is openly gay and in a gay marriage. This man believes God created him to be gay. The candidate is wrong. God created one man for one woman, as I have stated, but the Fall of Man allowed for all forms of sins to distort God's plan. Adam was created perfect until the Fall. After the Fall, all sorts of physical and mental diseases befell humanity. Yet, God will help those struggling with the weakness of homosexuality and other sins. He can find a way to overcome what Satan has corrupted.

"But remember this—the wrong desires that come into your life aren't anything new and different. Many others have faced exactly the same problems before you. And no temptation is irresistible. You can trust God to keep the temptation from becoming so strong that you can't stand up against it, for he has promised this and will do what he says. He will show you how to escape temptation's power so that you can bear up patiently against it." 1 Corinthians 10:13

Another justification used in defense of homosexuality is that the Old Testament allows all sorts of "prohibited" marriage, including polygamy, and what would today qualify as incest. If those were permitted, surely monogamous same-sex relationships should be allowed.[12, 13]

But the Old Testament is specific,

"You shall not lie with a male as with a woman; it is an abomination." Leviticus 18:22, NKJV

"If a man lies with a male as with a woman, both of them have committed an abomination; they shall surely be put to death; their blood is upon them." Leviticus 20:13

Just because these acts occurred does not mean God approved of them.

Here is another example of the LGBTQ community trying to justify itself as being right with God. Here is what their community says about Galatians 3:23-29. "This famous passage from Galatians is used in many contexts to sound the Christian call of unity in the face of division and difference. In fact, most of the Book of Galatians is an instruction to early Christians to embrace Gentile Christ-followers, even though they did not share in other early believers' Jewish history, tradition, or laws.

"Paul makes clear in these verses and elsewhere that Christ's promise is abundant and available to all people, and that those divisions and prejudices that have historically kept groups of people apart or given some power to some over others have no place in Christ's community. The particular phrase, *"there is no longer male and female,"* offers a challenge to traditional binary understandings of gender roles."[14]

But the LGBTQ community's above attempt at justification is utterly absurd. Only a person with the need to have this be true could believe the interpretation. Here is how the scripture actually reads,

"But before faith came, we were kept under guard by the law, kept for the faith which would afterward be revealed. 24 Therefore the law was our tutor *to bring us* to Christ, that we might be justified by faith. 25 But after faith has come, we are no longer under a tutor.

26 For you are all sons of God through faith in Christ Jesus. 27 For as many of you as were baptized into Christ have put on Christ. 28 There is neither Jew nor Greek, there is neither slave nor free, there is neither male nor female; for you are all one in Christ Jesus. 29 And if you *are* Christ's, then you are Abraham's seed, and heirs according to the promise." Galatians 3:23-29

The meaning is clear. All who believe in the Lord and repent are saved. This does not mean that they can say God approves of their former or present sin. Christians cannot compromise with Sin. But we love the sinner.

Of course, these and a hundred other different arguments are rationalizations used to justify behavior. I understand that human beings, because of the fall of Adam, have the lust of the flesh that leads to all types of sexual immorality—homosexuality and lesbianism being a part of that condition. But every person has free will and a choice to reject the sin.

Contrary to the belief of some, Born-again Christians do not hate people in the LGBTQ community. We love all people because Jesus died for the Sin of the whole World. However, we do not wish to embrace and accept this lifestyle as normal human behavior. Nor do we want to endorse it. Nor should we be forced to participate and encourage it by supporting gay marriage and rendering services that disagree with our beliefs.

Let us examine what the Scripture really says about this Sin. Which, by the way, I believe to be equally as wrong as gossip, lying, and slough. God's first command to Mankind was, *"Be fruitful and multiply...*" Practicing a homosexual lifestyle cannot produce life. God does not change.

> "Jesus Christ is the same yesterday and today and forever." Hebrews 13:8

Here are other Scriptures about Homosexuality in the New Testament, Paul writes in Romans.

> "So God let them go ahead into every sort of sexual sin, and do whatever they wanted to—yes, vile and sinful things with each other's bodies. [25] Instead of believing what they knew was the truth about God, they deliberately chose to believe lies. So they prayed to the things God made, but wouldn't obey the blessed God who made these things.
>
> [26] That is why God let go of them and let them do all these evil things, so that even their women turned against God's natural plan for them and indulged in sexual sin with each other. [27] And the men, instead of having normal sexual relationships with women, burned with lust for each other, men doing shameful things with other men and, as a result, getting paid within their own souls with the penalty they so richly deserved.
>
> [28] So it was that when they gave God up and would not even acknowledge him, God gave them up to doing everything their evil minds could think of." Romans 1:24-28

These acts create substantial health risks for those who advocate and practice licentious behaviors. Such are the dangers of Sin. [15]

And again in 1 Corinthians,

> "Those who live immoral lives, who are idol worshipers, adulterers or homosexuals—will have no share in his Kingdom. Neither will thieves or greedy people, drunkards, slanderers, or robbers." I Corinthians 6:9-10, Living Bible.

This doesn't mean there is no hope. God is merciful to those who repent and accept His Son. Paul immediately writes,

> "There was a time when some of you were just like that but now your sins are washed away, and you are set apart for God, and he has accepted you because of what the Lord Jesus Christ and the Spirit of our God have done for you." 1st Corinthians 6:11.

Christians are obligated to hate Sin but love the sinner. This does not mean we should condone and support their actions or their demands to be legitimized into acceptability. Christians must oppose political candidates who support the LGBTQ's legitimacy. God wishes salvation for all men, so we must treat them with love but refuse to validate their actions as normal and acceptable. Christian must vote for candidates who will not legitimize the LGBTQ community.

The Defense of the Nation of Israel must be a prime consideration for any major nation. As Moses writes in Deuteronomy 32 about God's purpose at the Tower of Babel.

> "When the Most High divided their inheritance to the nations, When He separated the sons of Adam, He set the boundaries of the peoples according to the number of the [c]children of Israel. For the LORD's portion is His people; Jacob is the place of His inheritance." Deuteronomy 32:8-9, NKJV.

God disowned all nations He would create in the future except the nation of Israel. You may say, "But there was no Jacob nor were there 'children of Israel' at the time of the Tower of Babel. But He had them created in His mind's eye. God is omnipresent. He is everywhere in every age at once and knew us from before the foundation of the World. He chose Abraham before Abram was even born.

From the time God called Abram, the nations that came from him were already blessed.

> *"Now the LORD had said to Abram: "Get out of your country, from your family and from your father's house, to a land that I will show you. I will make you a great nation; I will bless you and make your name great, And you shall be a blessing. I will bless those who bless you, And I will curse him who curses you; And in you, all the families of the earth shall be blessed."* Genesis 12:1-3.

What land did God instruct Abraham to go and promise to him? In Genesis 15, God puts Abraham to sleep and makes an everlasting covenant with him, defining the borders of the land He is giving him.

> *"To your descendants, I have given this land, from the river of Egypt to the great river, the River Euphrates—"* Genesis 15:18

At Bethel, God spoke to Jacob in a dream. He confirmed his promise to Abraham. And the Lord identified the genetic line the promise follows.

"*At the top of the stairs stood the Lord. "I am Jehovah," he said, "the God of Abraham, and of your father, Isaac. The ground you are lying on is yours! I will give it to you and to your descendants. [14] For you will have descendants as many as dust! They will cover the land from east to west and from north to south, and all the nations of the earth will be blessed through you and your descendants. [15] What's more, I am with you, and will protect you wherever you go and will bring you back safely to this land; I will be with you constantly until I have finished giving you all I am promising."* Genesis 28:13-15.

Genesis 28 nullifies any claim the Ishmaelites and succeeding nations springing from their lineage have on the promise. And yet, the people of Israel have never occupied all the land God promised them. But they will during the Millennium reign of Christ.

All the promises made to Abraham, Isaac, and Jacob and their descendants have come to pass except for the full control over the land and the End Times prophecies. As the time of the end approaches, the Bible is specific. Israel is the center point of the conflict.

> "For thus said the LORD of hosts, after his glory sent me to the nations who plundered you, for he who touches you touches the apple of his eye: "Behold, I will shake my hand over them, and they shall become plunder for those who served them. Then you will know that the LORD of hosts has sent me." Zechariah 2:8.

In our day, God has gathered Israel back from the four corners of the earth. He has made them a great nation. Any nation that raises its hand to destroy them will themselves be destroyed.

History proves scripture. Every nation that has conquered and enslaved the children of Israel has perished. Assyria, Babylon, the Persians, and the Medes, the Greeks, Romans, and Nazi Germany. They are no more. But Israel and the Jewish people still exist.

"...the LORD your God will bring you back from captivity, and have compassion on you, and gather you again from all the nations where the LORD, YOUR GOD, has scattered you.⁴ If any of you are driven out to the farthest parts under heaven, from there the LORD your God will gather you, and from there He will bring you.⁵Then the LORD your God will bring you to the land which your fathers possessed, and you shall possess it." Deuteronomy 30:3-5

This scripture was fulfilled during the 20ᵗʰ Century, and Jews have come from the four corners of the earth to settle in the land. Still, they are not believers on the Lord Jesus.

But Zechariah also predicted Israel will look upon Jesus and repent.

"Then I will pour out the spirit of grace and prayer on all the people of Jerusalem. They will look on him they pierced, and mourn for him as for an only son, and grieve bitterly for him as for an oldest child who died. ¹¹ The sorrow and mourning in Jerusalem at that time will be even greater than the grievous mourning for the godly King Josiah, who was killed in the valley of Megiddo. Zechariah 12:10-11

Daniel was shown the world of today before his death.

"Go your way, Daniel, for the words are closed up and sealed till the time of the end. ¹⁰Many shall be purified, made white, and refined, but the wicked shall do wickedly; and none of the wicked shall understand, but the wise shall understand...¹³ "But you, go your way till the end; for you shall rest, and will arise to your inheritance at the end of the days." Daniel 12:9-13.

Jews have returned to Israel since the end of World War II. God has blessed them, as He said he would. They are *'the apple of his eye.'* He made a promise as to the land they are to occupy. It does not belong to the Palestinians, the Arabs, or any other tribe of people. It is Israel's land by Godly decree. The United States must support and protect them, or we will fall like all the other powers that go against God.

"This is the fate of Israel, as pronounced by the Lord, who stretched out the heavens, laid the foundation of the earth, and formed the spirit of man within him:
² "I will make Jerusalem and Judah like a cup of poison to all the nearby nations that send their armies to surround Jerusalem. ³ Jerusalem will be a heavy stone burdening the world. And though all the nations of the

earth unite in an attempt to move her, they will all be crushed." Zechariah 12:1-3

A Christian voter must cast a ballot for those candidates who are pledged by their actions and/or past record to support the State of Israel, for they are still *'the apple of God's eye.'*

Immigration? Could the Bible hold a position regarding immigration? Yes. Americans are all immigrants or descendants of immigrants. Even the Indian tribes migrated across the Bering Strait thousands of years ago. God's law requires that we treat strangers and foreigners among us equally but with conditions. Moses directed his people in this manner,

> "GOD, your God, is the God of all gods, he's the Master of all masters, a God immense and powerful and awesome. He doesn't play favorites, takes no bribes, makes sure orphans and widows are treated fairly, takes loving care of foreigners by seeing that they get food and clothing.

19-21 You must treat foreigners with the same loving care—remember, you were once foreigners in Egypt." Deuteronomy 10:18-21, NIV.

It seems to me that, Biblically, there are two central issues as to how the Bible views immigration. Christians are to treat sojourners with love. But we are also obligated to maintain order in our society. Law and order are mandatory per Moses and the Ten Commandments.

To emphasize that order is an essential part of human society, I refer to Genesis 6.

But Noah was a pleasure to the Lord. Here is the story of Noah: **9-10** He was the only truly righteous man living on the earth at that time. He tried always to conduct his affairs according to God's will. And he had three sons—Shem, Ham, and Japheth.

11 Meanwhile, the crime rate was rising rapidly across the earth, and, as seen by God, the world was rotten to the core.

12-13 As God observed how bad it was, and saw that all mankind was vicious and depraved, he said to Noah, "I have decided to destroy all mankind; for the earth is filled with crime because of man. Yes, I will destroy mankind from the earth." Genesis 6:9-13, Living Bible.

God saved the just from the unjust and started over. His rules show His love for us. His justice separates His people from those who would corrupt us. Lawbreakers corrupt and destroy order and therefore are condemned. To accept people among us who violate God's laws and statutes is grave disobedience.

Here is a critical example in Exodus.

> "For these seven days there must be no trace of yeast in your homes; during that time anyone who eats anything that has yeast in it shall be excommunicated from the congregation of Israel. These same rules apply to foreigners who are living among you just as much as to those born in the land." Exodus 12:19

The word 'foreigner' is the same word for 'sojourner.' Verse 19 forbids eating anything with leaven. If anyone does, whether a sojourner or native-born, that person must be cut off from the congregation of Israel. This implies that the sojourner has become part of the flock of Israel and assimilated. A person cannot be cut off from a congregation of which they are not a part—first, they must have been a part of the congregation of Israel.

Deuteronomy reflects the same concept.

> "All of you—your leaders, the people, your judges, and your administrative officers—are standing today before the Lord your God, [11] along with your little ones and your wives and the foreigners that are among you—those who chop your wood and carry your water. [12] You are standing here to enter into a contract with Jehovah your God, a contract he is making with you today. [13] He wants to confirm you today as his people and to confirm that he is your God, just as he promised your ancestors, Abraham, Isaac, and Jacob. [14-15] This contract is not with you alone as you stand before him today, but with all future generations of Israel as well." Deuteronomy 29:10-15.

Foreigners were included in the pact because they accepted the Lord God of Israel.

Clearly, Christians are to love those who dwell among us, but there is also an order to be maintained. Immigrants must honor our way of life and accept our laws and statutes.

In the Old Testament, Ruth and Rahab found their way into the lineage of Christ by believing in the

God of Abraham, Isaac, and Jacob though they were Canaanite and Moabite gentiles. But when Esau went and took wives from the same peoples, he disgraced his family.

> "Esau, at the age of forty, married a girl named Judith, daughter of Be-eri the Hittite; and he also married Basemath, daughter of Elon the Hittite. [35] But Isaac and Rebekah were bitter about his marrying them. Genesis 26:34-35.

What is the difference? Esau and his wives raised a nation in rebellion to the Lord God. The Edomites became close relatives of other Levantine Semites. They worshiped such gods as El, Baal, Qaus, and Asherah. And the Hittite worshipped a thousand gods and led the people of Israel away from the Lord.

Their sin caused them to go into captivity, and they were commanded not to repeat the error when they returned from Babylon.

> "Now then make confession to the LORD, the God of your fathers and do his will. Separate yourselves from

the peoples of the land and from the foreign wives." Ezra 10:11

Many Scriptures point to loving and caring for the stranger and sojourner among us. These Scriptures apply to those who accept our culture and join with us in obeying God's laws and our nation's laws. But for those who commit crimes and bring confusion into our midst, they must be thrown out of our camp.

When voting, Christians should support legal immigration that follows our rules and statutes.

Also, the idea of sanctuary cities or states for lawbreakers is not Biblical. Illegal immigration is not Biblical. Biblical sanctuary cities worked together with law enforcement to protect due process of law. Sanctuary cities in America work against law enforcement to prevent due process of law.

"Tell the people of Israel to designate now the Cities of Refuge, as I instructed Moses. [3] If a man is guilty of killing someone unintentionally, he can run to one of these cities and be protected from the relatives of the dead man, who may try to kill him in revenge. [4] When the innocent killer reaches any of these cities, he will meet with the city council and explain what happened, and they must let him come in and must give him a place to live among them. [5] If a relative of the dead man comes to kill him in revenge, the innocent slayer must not be released to him for the death was accidental. [6] The man who caused the accidental death must stay in that city until he has been tried by the judges and found innocent and must live there until the death of the High Priest who was in office at the time of the accident. But then he is free to return to his own city and home." Joshua 20:2-6

In this example, the man who flees to a sanctuary city will face trial and, if found innocent, remains free. If found guilty, he must suffer the penalty. Not so in America.

The Biblical viewpoint on immigration is clear. Accept people who embrace our culture and follow our laws. Put those who do not hold to our culture or obey our laws out of our country. Do not support candidates that encourage or favor illegal immigration or sanctuary cities.

Can Humanity Save the Environment?

The complexity of today's environmental issues

presents a conflict in the minds of many Christians. The Bible sides with the environmentalists in that ever since The Fall, all creation has been dying. But the Bible disagrees with the idea that mankind has any solution to fix the problem. In fact, humanity is the problem.

God's resolve when creating humans was never to have us rely upon ourselves. But to trust in Him for everything. He wished to provide us with all we need by His grace, and we were to lovingly tend His creation.

> "So God created man in His own image; in the image of God He created him; male and female He created them. [28] Then God blessed them, and God said to them, "Be fruitful and multiply; fill the earth and subdue it; have dominion over the fish of the sea, over the birds of the air, and over every living thing that moves on the earth." Genesis 1:27-28, NKJV.

In the original state in which God fashioned Adam and Eve, human reasoning and problem solving were designed to operate within God's plan, not in Man's own strength. God instructed Man, and

Man watched over God's creation following God's commands. Everything God made worked fine as it was. He provided, educated, and guided all creation. He put Man in charge of seeing to the details of the design by following His instructions.

Then came the Fall. What had been easy for mankind turned into hard work and toil. Because of the Sin of Adam, nature inherited a curse. Perfect creation turned to imperfection, and the earth began to decay. Everything Man has devised to salvage or slow the breakdown of nature's balance ends up increasing the problems. Look at the Dust Bowl Era. Farmers did not consider the value of the root system of native plants and converted the ground to deep earth plowing. They removed the natural order that survived with little rain and replaced native plants with plants that could not survive with little rain. The deep ground plowing caused the Dust Bowl.[16]

The deforestation of the rainforests shows us that greed and poverty play a considerable part in the destruction of the Earth. On this issue, science has the means to reverse the decline of the rainforests but has run into the problem of the redistribution of wealth. Most rainforests are in impoverished countries and remote locations. It is up to the rich countries to fund the poor countries to accomplish the task of restoration. That means shutting down the timber and mining industries that generate wealth in the short term. As of the writing, there has been much talk but little action. In one hundred years, the rainforests will be gone.[17]

The love for the Florida Everglades has become its downfall. Starting in the early 20th Century, urban development and a misunderstanding of the natural water flow system destroyed much of the former Everglades. Today, Everglades National Park is working hard to preserve twenty-five percent of what was the original ecosystem.

Mankind made each situation worse through greed or thinking they could make it better.

> "For all creation is waiting patiently and hopefully for that future day when God will resurrect his children. [20-21] For on that day thorns and thistles, sin, death, and decay—the things that overcame the world against its will at God's command—will all disappear, and the world around us will share in the glorious freedom from sin which God's children enjoy.
> [22] For we know that even the things of nature, like animals and plants, suffer in sickness and death as they await this great event." Romans 8-19-22

Adam's fall affected the whole creation. Only by the return of Jesus, our Savior, with the Saints following, will Nature be returned to what it was at the time of Adam. This is the dilemma I have with reason-based solutions to environmental problems. Rational answers do not work. With all our knowledge, we still fall far short of God's wisdom and purpose.

111

Sadly, the Bible states emphatically, only Jesus' return can save our planet.

> "The earth mourns and fades away. The world languishes and fades away.
>
> The haughty people of the earth languish. 5The earth is also defiled under its inhabitants, because they have transgressed the laws, changed the ordinance, broken the everlasting covenant. 6Therefore the curse has devoured the earth,
>
> And those who dwell in it are desolate. Therefore, the inhabitants of the earth are burned, and few men are left. Isaiah 24:4-6, NIV.

This prophecy depicts the time just before our Lord returns. Jesus said the same in Matthew.

> "And there will be famines, pestilences, and earthquakes in various places. [8] All these are the beginning of sorrows... For then there will be great tribulation, such as has not been since the beginning of the world until this time, no, nor ever shall be. [22] And unless those days were shortened, no flesh would be saved; but for the elect's sake those days will be shortened." Matthew 24:7-8, 21-22, NKJV.

Given Man's greed, although I support efforts to protect and preserve wildlife and vegetation, mankind is incapable of making global improvements. We are fallen beings with no knowledge of God's plan. My advice is to concentrate on issues that will further the gospel and save people's souls.

Education and the Public Schools today leave much to be desired. The philosophies of the far left have gradually seeped down from the ivory towers of

America's colleges and universities and embedded in our public schools. Liberal-minded educators and school boards increasing attack freedom of religious expression and Conservative ideology.

The Left uses its ideas of social injustice and discrimination to attack football coaches as being offensive when kneeling in prayer on the field.[18] They attempt to remove God from the classroom and attack even the Second Lady of the United States for accepting a position in a Christian school that prohibits the LGBTQ community from teaching there.[19]

In the extreme, Antifa supporters use the word 'fascist' for anyone who disagrees with them and claims racist/fascist people have no right to freedom of speech. These terms are used to shut up opposition and silence debate. Instead of presenting their side with relevant plans and information, they shout down the opposition using words like homophobic, xenophobic, racist, and fascist.

The original Fascist Manifesto and the original Communist Manifesto sound remarkably the same in intent as the Antifa rhetoric. Government control, shared wealth, and confiscation of private and church property are fundamental tenets of all three ideologies. Revolutionaries and reactionaries go so far to the extreme that they end up in the same place with totalitarian governments.[20,21]

In the education arena, these anti-Christian/anti-Capitalist ideas are growing. As professors and teachers skew facts and impose their ideologies on our children. History itself is being systematically altered. Adolf Hitler once stated, "Give me a child when he's 7, and he's mine forever." Karl Marx is quoted often. *"Die Religion ... ist das Opium des Volkes"* and is often rendered as "religion... is the opiate of the masses." "Religion is the opium of the people" is one of the most frequently paraphrased statements of this German philosopher and economist.[20, 21]

Hitler was a fascist. Marx was a communist. Both arrive at the same place with anti-Christian and anti-Capitalist philosophies aimed at total government control of the people. Take away our freedoms a little piece at a time, and one day, we will wake up in a totalitarian state. Hitler also said, "Through the clever and constant application of propaganda, people can be made to see paradise as hell, and also the other way around, to consider the most wretched sort of life as paradise."[21]

Why should Christian parents pay for a public school system that bans God out of political correctness?

Regarding the pre-college education of our children, the state and local governments have the responsibility, not the federal government. Currently, over ninety-two percent of public-school funding comes from state and local funds, primarily property tax. Beware of accepting federal government assistance, federal funds hold out a carrot and a stick. The conditions for receiving them are wrapped in rules, regulations, and measurements that outweigh the financial benefits. Vote against federal programs where possible or elect local officials who will.

If you are politically active, propose legislation where your tax dollars can be directed toward the school you send your children, and encourage private schools and homeschool education programs, avoiding public education if possible.

As to higher education, why would a born-again, spirit-filled Christians want to send their children to the University of California-Berkeley, or Harvard, or Yale when these schools are blatantly ultra-left? Put your money to better use for God and your children by sending them to colleges and universities that respect work ethic and godly values. Schools like College of the Ozarks where students work to earn their tuition and can graduate debt-free. Pepperdine, which ranks above many Ivy League schools and, does not permit drinking on campus.

Research colleges and universities and select schools that align with your faith and still provide an excellent education. Here are some websites with lists of schools worth exploring if my children were college age.[22, 23]

There are many Christian Colleges and Universities to look at. The websites I listed are but a few of many choices. For useful reference material, check out Christian Universities online. Once you have selected a few that fit, go to U.S. News Best College Rankings and see how they rank academically.

Remember, if you attack the purse strings of activist organizations and use your vote effectively, you can hold off Satan's attack on our country and our children.

Chapter 9

The Power of the Purse! Make the term *follow the money* your beacon light. Christians make poor decisions daily about where they spend the Lord's money. Without researching the companies we buy products from, we unwittingly support causes we morally oppose. Check out *Investing Advice Watchdog* and *Faith Driven Consumer* as well as other watchdog websites to make judgments as to whether a company should be supported by your dollars.[24]

Christians should educate themselves about what companies donate their money to support and where their advertising dollars go. Corporations that put their money toward Anti-Christian programs should not receive Christian financial support. Check out free press articles on how corporations spend their advertising dollars and on which social programs they support.

Doing a thorough web search may add other sites to help you make educated purchasing choices. Writing down advertisers sponsoring wholesome programming is usually a safe bet. Companies, like people, put their dollars where their beliefs are.

With due diligence, a good researcher can find out what businesses donate the most money to various liberal and progressive programs. Companies that contribute to Planned Parenthood, for instance, can be found by searching the web for *Planned Parenthood's biggest donors*.[25]

There will be times when you have no good choices. But where you have an opportunity, go with organizations that support Biblical principles. At the time of this writing, these corporations ranked highest in holding to their Christian beliefs. [26]

1. Chick-fil-A
2. Forever 21
3. Tyson Foods

4. In-N-Out Burger

5. Interstate Batteries

6. Trijicon

7. Hobby Lobby

8. Service Master (Owns Merry Maid, Terminix, and American Home Shield.)

9. Mary Kay

10. H.E.B. Grocers

11. Carl's Jr.

12. Anschutz Entertainment Group

Chapter 10.

My Final Thoughts. Test the subjects I have covered. Look up the Scriptures and the context in which they were recorded. Pray for God's guidance, and study things out for yourself. Consider God's Word as a precious gift. Learn from the Word and compare the world today to what is written. Above all, love one another in Christ. Pray for those who are rejecting the Word of God that their eyes may be opened. Do no harm!

Remember, all of us born of a human father are sinners, and we do not deserve eternal joy or happiness. Only by the grace of God, we are saved. I consider myself like Paul, the worst of sinners saved by grace.

Do not judge politicians by their looks or their rhetoric. Judge them by whether they align themselves with the Word of God in their decisions for America. Study the lies of the devil and his tactics.

He and those under his control will not admit their faults. They will deflect and minimize them, project greater shortcomings on others, and explode visions beyond their capabilities to achieve them.

Put your finances to work for good, not evil. Be bold in your defense of the gospel of Jesus Christ. The Body of Christ has power. Jesus said,

> "Most assuredly, I say to you, he who believes in Me, the works that I do he will do also; and greater works than these he will do because I go to My Father." John 14:12.

We have the authority. And there has never been a better time in the history of Man that we need to demonstrate the power He has given us. Prepare yourself so you can say as Paul said,

> "For I am already being poured out as a drink offering, and the time of my departure is at hand. ⁷ I have fought the good fight, I have finished the race, I have kept the faith. ⁸ Finally, there is laid up for me the crown of righteousness, which the Lord, the righteous Judge, will give to me on that Day, and not to me only but also to all who have loved His appearing. 2 Timothy 6-8

The End

XI. Appendix

1. https://www.people-press.org/2018/08/09/an-examination-of-the-2016-electorate-based-on-validated-voters/

2. CNN Exit poll https://www.cnn.com/election/2016/results/exit-polls

3. NBC https://www.nbcnews.com/politics/2016-election/president

4. New York Times/National Election Pool https://www.nytimes.com/interactive/2016/11/08/us/politics/election-exitpolls.html

5. https://www.npr.org/2018/05/21/612844060/election-night-shakeup-here-come-the-new-exit-polls

6. F.F. Bruce quote. https://www.azquotes.com/author/22836-F_F_Bruce

7. Farrakhan https://www.jpost.com/Diaspora/Farrakhan-compares-Jews-totermites-says-Jews-are-stupid-569627

8. Ilhan Omar https://www.nytimes.com/2019/03/07/opinion/ilhan-omaranti-semitism.html

9. https://www.carprousa.com/4th-Of-July-Quotes-From-Our-Founding-Fathers/a/908

10. Church of England/Government *www.history.com/topics/britishhistory/church-of-england.*

11. https://www.abc.net.au/news/2017-08-23/same-sex-marriage-what-biblehas-to-say-robyn-whitaker/8831826

12. The Bible And Same-sex Marriage: 6 Common But Mistaken .., https://bible.org/article/bible-and-same-sex-marriage-6-common-mistakenclaims.

13. Queer Bible Hermetics https://blog.smu.edu/ot8317/2016/05/11/leviticus-1822/

14. https://sojo.net/articles/10-bible-passages-teach-christian-perspective-homosexuality

15. The Dust Bowl https://en.wikipedia.org/wiki/Dust_Bowl

16. Rainforests https://www.theguardian.com/global-developmentprofessionals-network/2017/jan/23/destroying-rainforests-quickly-gone-100years-deforestation

17. https://en.wikipedia.org/wiki/Restoration_of_the_Everglades

18. https://www.usatoday.com/story/news/politics/2019/01/22/supreme-courtwont-hear-praying-football-coach-case/1943694002/
19. http://time.com/5504621/karen-pence-backlash-christianschool-lgbtq/
20. Hitler http://bit.ly/2Vd7hOw

21. Marx https://en.wikiquote.org/wiki/Karl_Marx

22. Christian Universities
    https://www.christianuniversitiesonline.org/bestchristian-colleges/
23. https://www.crosswalk.com/special-coverage/higher-education/best-christian-colleges-universities.html

24. http://www.investingadvicewatchdog.com/LiberalCompanies-Boycott.html

25. http://www.faithdrivenconsumer.com/

26. https://www.opensecrets.org/outsidespending/contrib.php?cmte=Planned+Parenthood&cycle=2018

27. Dr. Rabbi David Frankel, October 28, 2016, The Torah,
    https://www.thetorah.com/article/noah-ham-and-the-curse-ofcanaan-who-did-what-to-whom-in-the-tent

References:

Edward G. Lengel. Charlottesville: University of Virginia Press, 2006, p. 13.]
"General Orders, 2 May 1778," *Founders Online,* National Archives, accessed
April 11, 2019, https://founders.archives.gov/documents/Washington/03-1502-
0016. [Original source: *The Papers of George Washington*, Revolutionary War
Series, vol. 15, *May–June 1778,* ed.

J. Jefferson Looney. Princeton: Princeton University Press, 2009, pp. 236–23
"John Adams to Thomas Jefferson, 28 June 1813," Founders Online, National
Archives, accessed April 11, 2019,
https://founders.archives.gov/documents/Jefferson/03-06-02-0208. [Original
source: The Papers of Thomas Jefferson, Retirement Series, vol. 6, 11 March to
27 November 1813, ed. 9.]

John Hancock. (n.d.). AZQuotes.com. Retrieved August 21,2019, from
AZQuotes.com Website https://www.azquotes.com/quote/1057441

Benjamin Franklin wrote this in a letter to Ezra Stiles, President of Yale
University, on March 9, 1790.

Robyn J Whitaker, Bromby Lecturer in Biblical Studies, Trinity College, University
of Divinity, quote in https://theconversation.com/to-christiansarguing-no-on-
marriage-equality-the-bible-is-not-decisive-82498

Layton E Williams. June 6, 2017, Sojourners, Article "10 Passages that Teach a
Christian Perspective on Homosexuality. https://sojo.net/articles/10-
biblepassages-teach-christian-perspective-homosexuality.

JESSICA MARTINEZ AND GREGORY A. SMITH, NOVEMBER
9, 2016, How the faithful voted: A preliminary 2016 analysis
https://www.pewresearch.org/fact-tank/2016/11/09/how-the-faithfulvoted-a-
preliminary-2016-analysis/

NBC, November 9, 2016,
https://www.nbcnews.com/politics/2016election/president

CNN, November 9, 2016, Political News Team
https://www.cnn.com/election/2016/results/exit-polls.

Walter C. Kaiser, Jr., Peter H. Davids, F. F. Bruce, Manfred Brauch (2010). "Hard Sayings of the Bible," p.364, InterVarsity Press.
https://www.azquotes.com/author/22836-F_F_Bruce

Jon Huang, SAMUEL JACOBY, MICHAEL STRICKLAND, and K.K. REBECCA LAI, November 8, 2016, New York Times Exit Polls
https:www.nytimes.com/interactive/2016/11/08/us/politics/election-exit-polls

Domenico Montanaro, May 21, 2018, NPR **Election Night Shakeup: Here Come The New 'Exit' Polls,**
https://www.npr.org/2018/05/21/612844060/election-night-shakeuphere-come-the-new-exit-polls

JEREMY SHARON, OCTOBER 17, 2018, JERUSALEM POST, FARRAKHAN COMPARES JEWS TO TERMITES, SAYS JEWS ARE 'STUPID.'
https://www.jpost.com/Diaspora/Farrakhan-compares-Jews-to-termitessays-Jews-are-stupid-569627
BRENT STEPHENS, MARCH 7, 2019 ILHAN OMAR KNOWS WHAT SHE'S DOING, HTTPS://WWW.NYTIMES.COM/2019/03/07/OPINION/ILHAN-OMAR-ANTI-SEMITISM

John Adams, *Diary and Autobiography*, 3:233-34, Build Upon the Rock: John Quincy Adams' Letters on the Bible and Its Teachings,
https://christianhertiagefellowship.com/Christian-quotes-from-the-foundingfathers.

Darrell L. Bock, 7/27/2015, The Bible and Same-Sex Marriage: 6 Common But Mistaken Claims https://bible.org/article/bible-and-same-sex-marriage-6common-mistaken-claims

Anonymous Student, 05/11/2016, Queer Bible Hermetics
https://blog.smu.edu/ot8317/2016/05/11/leviticus-1822/

Financial Investing: http://www.investingadvicewatchdog.com/LiberalCompanies-Boycott.html

Gregory, N. James. (1991) *American Exodus: The Dust Bowl Migration and Okie Culture in California*. Oxford University Press. The Dust Bowl-Wiki.

John Vidal, Jan. 23, 2017 https://www.theguardian.com/global-developmentprofessionals-network/2017/jan/23/destroying-rainforests-quickly-gone-100years-deforestation

Dovell, Junius (July 1948). "The Everglades: A Florida Frontier," *Agricultural History* **22** (3), pp. 187–197. The Restoration of the Everglades, Wikipedia

Richard Ward, (January 2019) https://www.usatoday.com/story/news/politics/2019/01/22/supreme-courtwont-hear-praying-football-coach-case/1943694002/

KATIE REILLY, JANUARY 16, 2019, TIME, https://time.com/5504621/karen-pence-backlash-christian-school-lgbtq/

KUSD, December 28, 2015. Website can not be found.

Karl Marx *A Contribution to the Critique of Hegel's Philosophy of Right*, published after Marx death. Wiki quotes.

Chelsea Schilling, World Net Dailey, 12/1/2016, https://www.wnd.com/2016/12/47-u-s-companies-join-anti-trump-breitbartblacklist/

Open Secrets.Org. Based on data released by the FEC on June 10, 2019. https://www.opensecrets.org/outsidespending/contrib.php?cmte=Planned+Parenthood&cycle=2018

About the Author:

Thank you for purchasing *Christianity Faces the 21st Century, The Spirit, The Ballot Box, and the Pocketbook.* If you liked the book, please review it on Amazon. A few short sentences will offer your honest view of the writing and help others select a book they will enjoy. I write about the high-stress issues facing everyday Americans in the 21st Century. I'm into real-life endings. Media headlines plant the ideas that drive my creative side. I push the plots out a few years, predicting the outcomes inside the subplots of my novels, and thus far, I've been spot on. My motivation for writing stems from a desire to influence my readers' perceptions of the world in which they live and the issues humanity faces today. If you're looking for an author match, I've been compared to Robert Heinlein in writing style. Heinlein was a great storyteller who refused to allow a setting to interfere with moving the plot along. He never wasted the reader's time with unfamiliar cultural trends or fancy words. Dialogue and snippets of exposition built the tension of his worlds with a minimum of effort. This is what I strive to do. I love meeting my readers. I want to hear from my readers. If you see me at a writers' conference, come up and say hello. Follow my blog at www.billwetterman.com and see what I am working on next. Tweet to me anytime at #BillWetterman. Share your thoughts and opinions with me. Email me at bwetterman@cox.net or go to my Facebook page and friend me at Author Bill Wetterman.

I look forward to hearing from you soon.

Made in the USA
Middletown, DE
06 October 2023

40362739R00078